KINGSBRIDGE

Etiquette

BY JOSH TOLLEY

KINGSBRIDGE

First edition 2023

Book layout and design by Josh Tolley

Hardcover ISBN: 978-1-7325985-3-9
E-book ISBN: 978-1-7325985-4-6

Published by Kingsbridge, LLC
www.JoshTolley.com

KINGSBRIDGE

KINGSBRIDGE

Kingsbridge Etiquette is a standard of etiquette and protocol based on the reality that the world, and particularly those involved in enterprise, need to return to a place of person-to-person interaction and social decorum, one of professional courtesy and personal development. Etiquette and protocol should be applied to all interactions, without bias, segregation, or exclusion.

Exercising etiquette is an expression of respect and honor towards others and also to yourself. When these practices become part of your foundational behavior, you will develop a higher standard of living in both a private life as well as a professional one. This is a luxury not tied to income, which cannot be confiscated, can comfort and also reward.

The points contained therein are manners of behavior that we encourage Kingsbridge staff to adopt into their professional and personal interactions and activities. We invite all organizations and communities wishing to implement measurable standards of betterment to employ Kingsbridge Etiquette as well.

KINGSBRIDGE

The betterment of human interaction benefits all interaction.

1

PURSUE EXCELLENCE IN ALL YOU DO

Whether it means exercising hard work before claiming 'expertise' or picking up the piece of trash that missed the disposal basket, never look for - or even accept - less than your potential.

KINGSBRIDGE

2

ELEVATE YOUR LANGUAGE

Continue to improve your grammar and vocabulary regularly. While improving, convey this improvement through better vocal and written communication. Avoid saying things like, "Yeah, I'd be up for that," when a better wording would phrase it as, "I would be honored to do so; thank you very much."

KINGSBRIDGE

3

SELECT THE HIGHEST QUALITY

Regardless of one's station in life, make it a practice to invest in the highest level of quality and service possible for your budget. It not only benefits society but it also makes life better, easier, more enjoyable, and less stressful. It typically saves money in the long run as well.

KINGSBRIDGE

4

ON ENTITLEMENT

You deserve less than what you believe you do; we all do. Therefore, make efforts to prevent a self-righteous and entitled perspective in life. Additionally, do not create imaginary obstacles where none exist. These behaviors look foolish to adults, and can ruin opportunities that would otherwise be open to you.

KINGSBRIDGE

5

OFFER REGAL SERVICE

When compromising on the service provided and the effort put into one's actions, not only are others robbed of the level of excellence they deserve, but you rob yourself of realizing your full potential in serving them. You should see yourself as a 5-star service provider in all you do and ask yourself constantly, "Am I performing at my own highest level and 'wowing' those I am serving?"

KINGSBRIDGE

6

DRESS HIGHER THAN THE MASSES

Even though the world seems to celebrate the billionaire in the hoodie, there is no denying that the more sophisticated the dress, the more respect is demanded by it; the more honor displayed to those with whom you are interacting, the higher the standard you will project in the community that observes you without you knowing.

KINGSBRIDGE

7

MEET IN PERSON

There is no substitute for live, in-person meetings. Even if an electronically-hosted meeting is offered, attempt to meet in-person instead. It keeps humanity connected, provides for better, interpersonal connections, increases results in desired outcomes, and also increases the ability to gather intelligence and understanding more than any other form of meeting can.

KINGSBRIDGE

8

ON VIDEO CONFERENCING

Do not attend video conferences while driving; instead, pull over. In addition to the technical problems the meeting will always suffer from a moving participant, it also causes a rude distraction. The same holds true for eating while on video: don't do it.

If you must attend a video call while in transit, turn off your camera so as to eliminate the surrounding distractions and reduce interruptions. Muting yourself as much as possible when background noise is present is also advised.

9

HONOR SKILLS OVER EDUCATION

A person should be proud of the work they put in completing their higher education; however, they should be prouder - and more honored by society - for the hard work they put into gaining experience and skills. As more employers are moving away from college degree requirements, it is important to make a point of honoring and rewarding real experience and skills over education.

KINGSBRIDGE

10

MASTER INTRODUCTIONS

When introducing people to each other, intentionally start with the persons who are not in your party, beginning with the highest person of station in the other party directed to the highest person of station in your party until each has been introduced.

When introducing your party, conduct the introductions in the same manner starting with your highest person of station first towards the highest person of station on the other side until each person has been introduced.

KINGSBRIDGE

11

REMOVE SUNGLASSES OR EARPHONES

When in conversation with someone in person, it is proper to remove your sunglasses and both earbuds. Not doing so is in poor taste and looks tacky.

KINGSBRIDGE

12

BRING A GIFT

When invited to meet with someone other than close friends and family, especially for the first time, it is always advisable to bring a gift. The gift does not need to be exorbitant. Affordable tokens that offer a personal touch to the recipient can actually have a more positive impact than an impersonal expensive gift.

KINGSBRIDGE

13

ON ANSWERING
THE PHONE

When in an appropriate situation, never answer the phone with just a "Hello?" It is more fitting to answer a call by saying, "Hello, this is _____ " or, "Hello, this is _____ speaking. How can I help you?" More words lead to a warmer conversation.

KINGSBRIDGE

14

WHEN USING THE PHONE

Be respectful of others as well as your caller when on the phone. If on speaker phone, let all parties know from the beginning the call is on speaker and announce who is listening. If not on speaker phone, excuse yourself from the presence of others and reserve all particulars for when you are in private. Also, request from your surrounding guests to grant you permission to take the call when your phone rings.

KINGSBRIDGE

15

REPLY WITH MORE THAN ONE WORD

Rather than replying with a simple "Please" or "Thanks", provide enough words to convey a sentiment; but not so many as to cause one to think of you as a "wind bag."

A few more words conveys a sense of honor and respect towards the person as well as a sincere acknowledgement of what he or she has said to you.

KINGSBRIDGE

16

ON VOICEMAIL

Voicemails should convey a simple message, not a conversation. Keep the message short; state your name, the topic you wish to discuss when they call back, and your preferred contact information, that's all. Leave the conversation for the conversation.

KINGSBRIDGE

17

RESPONDING PROMPTLY

It is not fitting to wait longer than 24 hours before responding to calls, emails, or personal letters. That includes replies that are just to inform the other party that you did indeed receive their message and will need to respond again in the future with a more complete message. Not only are prompt responses an example of good etiquette, but they will add productivity and opportunity to your life.

KINGSBRIDGE

18

ON DELIVERING BAD NEWS

On the off chance that the news you are to deliver is in the negative, deliver it in such a way whereas you acknowledge the impact it will have on the person(s) you are delivering it to. Also make sure to add a word of encouragement and the possibility for future good news to be provided thereafter.

KINGSBRIDGE

19

AVOID GOSSIP

It goes without saying that while the taste of gossip is sweet, the aftertaste is bitter. It is better to politely slip away from a conversation than to allow gossip to taint the airways.

KINGSBRIDGE

20

BE PERSONABLE, NOT PERSONAL

It is fine to engage in pleasantries and even to compliment another; however, avoid crossing over into a personal conversation or addressing personal topics with others until the other has invited you into that relationship status.

Do not pursue that invitation, either, as more often than not professional relationships that become too personal too quickly destroy both the professional and personal relationships altogether.

KINGSBRIDGE

21

ELIMINATE BACKGROUND NOISE

In a world where working from home is more common, family life behind a phone call is a reality. Make sure to eliminate the likelihood of pets or children being heard on the call. Though some can seemingly ignore the family noise and carry on a conversation, others cannot and should not. It is unprofessional to talk with anyone other than family and close friends while the noisy disturbance of children and pets is in the background.

KINGSBRIDGE

22

FILTER OPINIONS

Listen to others' opinions with a filter of deductive reasoning, not allowing yourself to be captivated by self-defined truth or emotionally-based positions. While people do matter, uninformed or emotionally based opinions do not and they can be a plague to civilization if too many people ally with toxic reasoning. This is why opinions must be filtered as to not cause any damage to self or to others.

KINGSBRIDGE

23

LIMIT WHAT IS COMMUNICATED

Don't over-share your life, hobbies, and especially problems with others with whom you have professional interactions. Keep these aspects of your life where they belong: in the confines of close friends and family.

KINGSBRIDGE

24

ON PRIVACY AND CONFIDENTIALITY

Everyone deserves to have their privacy and confidentiality respected. This goes beyond not blatantly spying and applies also to purposely turning away, exiting a room, ignoring conversation or other communications, such as correspondence, that doesn't apply to you.

KINGSBRIDGE

25

PRAISE IN PUBLIC, REBUKE IN PRIVATE

In the 'age of rage' where people love to point out others' faults, on-line especially, it must be remembered that people of value do not do such things. When a problem arises with a person or an organization, take it to them privately firstly, a network of their direct peers secondly, the courts if need thirdly, but avoid, when at all possible, publicizing faults, errors or misfortune, especially if you are to gain by their exposure. Keep matters as private as possible.

KINGSBRIDGE

26

NOT REFUSING A GIFT

Turning down a gift is not being polite; it is being rude. A rejection of a gift is a rejection of the giver. Accept gifts with gratitude and humility, making a point of honoring the giver when given the opportunity. If unsure as to whether or not you should open the gift at the moment of reception, ask the giver his or her preference.

KINGSBRIDGE

27

DO NOT CROWD

When waiting to board a form of transportation or waiting to enter any other means of access, do not crowd the point of entry. Also, never block an open entrance when there is an alternative option available. Find a spacious place to stand so others are more comfortable around you.

KINGSBRIDGE

28

DRIVE COURTEOUSLY

There is no excuse to become lazy in vehicular etiquette. When meeting a car at a four way stop, instead of waving the car on, the one on the right goes first. Upon encountering pedestrians, use logic and respect: no cutting people off in traffic, use turn signals, and be consciencious about open spaces.

It's the little things that matter when it comes to being a courteous driver and it goes without saying: put down the phone and the cosmetics.

KINGSBRIDGE

29

NOT CAUSING DISCOMFORT

Use caution in your interactions with objects that others may be using. For example, it is rude to kick the chair in front of you or use someone's seat to stand up if the person is still seated. Do not cause discomfort to others around you to service your own needs; look out for their needs first.

KINGSBRIDGE

30

PUNCTUALITY CONVEYS RESPECT

Always be punctual. When circumstances force a delay, convey that delay to the others involved as soon as you possibly can. Never excuse away or laugh off your tardiness whether it is rare or habitual. Respecting the other person's time and attention is of highest concern.

KINGSBRIDGE

31

WHEN DINING WITH OTHERS

Do not partake in your food before everyone else is served. The host, or honored party, must be provided an opportunity to address the attendees or, if their tradition, to say a blessing. Do not start eating or engaging in your meal until the highest-stationed person, or the honored party, begins eating first.

KINGSBRIDGE

32

TABLE ETIQUETTE

Study and practice proper table etiquette. This includes dabbing your mouth after taking a drink, shielding a lemon or lime when squeezing, passing dishes clockwise, not accepting or asking for leftovers in the company of acquaintances. These and many other points of etiquette should be practiced when dining with or without others.

KINGSBRIDGE

33

ON LUNCHEONS

A luncheon is a mid-day meal where the conversation, positioning, and objectives are more of an engagement for professional, strategic, or social purposes using dining as a base of connectivity.

While lunch can be enjoyed with lighthearted whimsey, a luncheon must be honored and respected with full deployment of manners and etiquette.

KINGSBRIDGE

34

WHEN OFFERING REFRESHMENTS

Offer refreshments to those in your company before accepting and partaking of the refreshments yourself. If your party is hosting, offer refreshments to your guests prior to offering them to your party, and make sure to participate in the exchange.

KINGSBRIDGE

35

DISTRACTIONS
AT THE TABLE

Whether engaged in refreshments or a meal, as long as others are present with you in conversation, there should be no distractions - including phones - when sitting with others. Make the person feel special by removing distractions.

KINGSBRIDGE

36

NO NEED FOR POLITICS

It may be enticing to bring political allegiances into an interaction. The truth is that politics are the focused and manipulated extension of one's beliefs.

When it comes to personal interactions, allow one's beliefs to be communicated topic by individual topic as that becomes a more strategic method of connecting on what is shared. This allows the _heart_ of one's political beliefs to be involved in discourse without the toxicity of political parties impacting the interaction. Besides, commerce is a larger and more permanent force than any political system or ideology, allowing commerce to bridge more beliefs overall.

KINGSBRIDGE

37

RESPECTING THE STATION

The term 'station' can be based on such things as: age, accomplishment, professional ranking, or other warranted differentiations.

When in the presence of someone of a higher station, respect him or her, their time, space and attention. For example, if you and someone of higher station need to slide into a booth, the person of lesser station should be the one to slide further, etc.

KINGSBRIDGE

38

STATE YOUR FULL NAME

When meeting someone for the first several times, always state your full name when introduced or asked. Do not use your first name by itself until the person of higher station offers his or her first name by itself. If you are the person of higher station, do not extend that invite for at least the first three meetings.

Allowing one to address you exclusively by your first name causes all parties to lower their social standards. Doing this before the proper time is not actually nice, it can eventually harm the relationship.

KINGSBRIDGE

39

EXPECT RESPECT

Too often, someone who has earned their station will yield their warranted respect because society has compromised this building block of social decorum for the sake of entitlement disguised as equality.

Compromising one's station can harm others more than help them. Rather, it is appropriate to provide others the opportunity and reason to rise to the occasion and better themselves through their practice of etiquette and protocol by showing proper respect to another in a higher station.

KINGSBRIDGE

40

AVOID EMBARRASSING OTHERS

When self-defined opinions and self-identifying actions don't match the truth or facts, the temptation arises to deliver correction in such a way that brings embarrassment to the one in error, especially if that error is founded on personal expression and emotion. While it temporarily feels pleasurable to correct and embarrass the self-identifying one, it can cause more damage to individuals and to society at large.

KINGSBRIDGE

41

SPECIAL, SECRET AND BIGGER THAN THEMSELVES

Every person wants three things in life. Always seek a way to make those you are interacting with feel special, be invited to be a part of something bigger than themselves, and be included in a "secret." (Even if the secret is nothing more than a level of trust between you.)

KINGSBRIDGE

42

CLEAN UP AFTER YOURSELF AND YOUR PARTY

Always leave a place better than you entered. This includes not leaving a popcorn tub behind in the movie theatre. This includes eliminating all evidence that your dog was present. Cleaning up after yourself and your party is essential.

KINGSBRIDGE

43

USE CASH WHEN POSSIBLE

Not only is cash much more intimate, it also provides opportunities for the receiver that are diminished when electronically-delivered funds are used.

KINGSBRIDGE

44

TIP,
AND TIP WELL

Tips should be thought of as an opportunity, not a "pay off." They are a token of "realized appreciation." This action has the potential to better people and communities directly and also provides a motivation for useful connection and opportunity which otherwise may not exist.

This does NOT apply when a tip is asked for, expected, or when prompted on an electronic device. Tipping in those cases should be avoided as the expectation and asking for the tip is rude.

KINGSBRIDGE

45

EMPOWER LOWER STATIONS

Station in life is not indicative of worth; all people are priceless. Make it a point to edify, empower, and complement people of lower station and seek to provide opportunity for advancement when proper . Someone of lower station should be honored and respected as much as someone of higher station. Interactions should not look the same, but honor and respect are never bound by station in life.

KINGSBRIDGE

46

FORGIVE THOSE WILLING TO CHANGE

Today the world is being deprived of greatness because society refuses to allow people to grow and change. As someone who practices etiquette and protocol, you have the ability to improve society by providing a path of redemption to those who have more to offer once the fresh water of forgiveness has been allowed to wash away the stain of past mistake.

KINGSBRIDGE

47

PRACTICE TOLERANCE BUT NEVER FORCE ACCEPTANCE

Everyone deserves respect and freedom. It is proper etiquette to tolerate all people, their ways of life and views. However, one must be very careful around evil-doers who suggest or enforce anyone to accept or promote a way of life contrary to their own. Forced acceptance and promotion breeds hatred and inequality.

KINGSBRIDGE

48

ON STATION AND SOCIAL MEDIA

On social media platforms such as Twitter and LinkedIn where professional communication is exchanged, feel free to follow people of higher and lower station than yourself. However, on other platforms with a more personal expression such as Instagram or Facebook, it is not fitting to follow people of higher or lower station who are in your professional circumstances without asking for permission to first. Not doing so blends lines that should not and would not normally be blended if there was not so much access into people's lives. The exception to this is if that person you wish to 'follow' are public figures.

KINGSBRIDGE

49

ON MORALITY

A morality decided by oneself is better termed as behavioral preferences. Morality must come from something higher than self, be it God, fraternity, logically-sound law, or anything other than solely oneself. Morality must measure up to someone else's standards that may not agree with your personal beliefs and preferences. Otherwise, you are not really a moral person, you are at high risk of becoming a self-affirming, self-serving blight upon humanity.

Living a moral life provides empowerment through confinement. If your morality allows you to do what you wish, when you wish; then you are a perfect example of an immoral person.

The objective over time is to be transformed by the confinement to a level of freedom and joy otherwise unattainable.

KINGSBRIDGE

50

ON TROLLING

Being a "troll" on-line or in-person is a form of antagonization via messaging that provides no positive outcome for anyone, even the troll. It actually shows a lack of maturity, lack of self-respect, and a lack of self-worth. Offer constructive communication or nothing at all.

KINGSBRIDGE

51

AVOID HIGH ESG, DEI & CEI SCORES

Instead of promoting responsible governance, environmentally sound practices, fairness, diversity, inclusion & equality, the ESG, DEI and CEI scores are being leveraged as a form of abuse to force compliance in order to gain access to capital and opportunity. They are now a leading cause *of hatred, division, subjugation, real inequality, societal decay, environmental endangerment, and poor business practices harming shareholders, stakeholders, customers and their communities.*

It makes long-term professional sense to avoid falling for the ESG/DEI/CEI scheme when it comes to professional operations. It is also proper etiquette to avoid investing business funds with firms that promote this toxicity. Pursue hesitancy in doing business with any company that promotes their ESG/DEI/CEI compliance or methods.

KINGSBRIDGE

52

HALT ATTACKERS

While broad and warranted ridicule can be embraced; focused and continued attacks cannot. First, try to reason: take the opportunity for polite conversation and settlement. If malicious attacks continue, the resulting consequences belong to the attacker, not the defender. Make a short but deliberate work of counterattacking which can eliminate further attacks. Allowing one to continue may not only destroy your opportunity to better the world, but it also endangers others by opening them up for attacks as well. Remember that the ways of the world today do not pursue any longer a society which seeks betterment, refinement, atonement and achievement, but rather hate, rage and self-centered emotional expression; so attackers must be halted.

KINGSBRIDGE

53

ONLINE COACHING AND MENTORSHIP

Offering on-line coaching as the main or a major source of income makes one look unprofessional. It also deprives the mentee from the real interactive benefits associated with and needed from true, in-person coaching and mentorship. Mentors and coaches should never derive more than 10% of their income from offering these services either.

A real mentor or coach should be deriving 90% of their income from actually practicing their area of expertise, not solely teaching it on-line.

KINGSBRIDGE

54

IN ALL YOUR GETTING, GET UNDERSTANDING

Make an effort to gain basic - if not also expert - knowledge and understanding of a broad array of topics in order to be prepared for any conversation. A wider framework helps to better understand others' points of view.

KINGSBRIDGE

55

THINK CRITICALLY, NOT CYNICALLY

Critical thinking is one of the keys to happiness. Too often people think they are being critical thinkers, but they are really just cynical. Cynicism leads to untold loss of opportunity, loss of trustworthiness, and while it might seem self-protecting and wise, it is really self-endangering and foolish.

KINGSBRIDGE

56

GIVE ADVICE
ONLY WHEN ASKED

When offering advice on what actions to take or what behaviors to employ, it is often not taken as helpful as it is intended to be. Instead, it looks boastful.

At the same time, offering unsolicited advice creates a situation where the recipient is actually less likely to take it and even less likely to open up to you again in order to prevent the rudeness from occurring again. Unless asked, or the permission has already been established in the relationship, never give unsolicited advice. Facts and data, though, can almost always be provided and can prove to be more helpful both to people and relationships.

KINGSBRIDGE

57

EMBRACE RIDICULE

When standing up for what is right, many will attempt to attack. Do not apologize for proper behavior; instead embrace the fact that people of lower station and lesser maturity will often act out of emotion and/or poor assumption. Those of equal and greater station who have gained wisdom and maturity do not engage in such foolishness. Offer explanations to those of merit not to those of pity or contempt.

58

USE DEDUCTIVE REASONING

Self-defined truth is rarely true and their is no such thing as "your" truth. This demeaning foolishness is usually based on desire, preference, or emotion - three things that should never be present when determining truth. Use deductive reasoning, ask questions, and gain knowledge to determine the objective truth of a matter so as to avoid pride, arrogance, a sense of undeserved entitlement and fault.

59

BE HUMBLE IN VICTORY AND DEFEAT

A defeated foe or a victor may prove to be a great alliance if given the opportunity. Pride blinds the foolish from spotting opportunities which may form such beneficial relationships. Remain humble at all times so as to not miss out on such opportunities.

KINGSBRIDGE

60

LIVE THE LOGICAL LIFE

Whether a person of faith or a practitioner of the stoic methods, there is no doubt that a logically-guided life is one that offers deep happiness, success, and higher fulfillment.

The Logical Life ™ is comprised of four rules, nine pillars, and eight guideposts which can assist in the journey from **success** to **significance**.

www.LiveTheLogicalLife.com

KINGSBRIDGE

KINGSBRIDGE

JOSH TOLLEY

Josh Tolley is the founder and chairman of Tolley and Company - a privately held collection of companies which includes the Kingsbridge collection of business services.

Josh Tolley has been featured in print, television, and radio interviews around the world for his business and leadership skills.

www.JoshTolley.com

KINGSBRIDGE

Kingsbridge is a Strategic GM&A (Growth, Mergers, and Acquistions) firm offering multiple services to privately held companies around the world, including: brokerage, interest- free financing, accounting, deal sourcing, growth partnerships, strategic planning, and the proprietary T.I.P.S.S. Index.

Additionally, Kingsbridge provides products and services such as Kingsbridge Etiquette and the Kingsbridge KESI system as well as educating the public on the power of privately-controlled companies and responsible economic policy.

www.KingsbridgeBrokers.com

KINGSBRIDGE

where business reigns